GW00457961

Gallery Books
Editor Peter Fallon
THIS ONE HIGH FIELD

Michelle O'Sullivan

THIS ONE HIGH FIELD

17·10·18

Gallery Books

This One High Field
is first published
simultaneously in paperback
and in a clothbound edition
on 17 October 2018.

The Gallery Press
Loughcrew
Oldcastle
County Meath
Ireland

www.gallerypress.com

ISBN 978 1 91133 753 9 *paperback*
978 1 91133 754 6 *clothbound*

A CIP catalogue record for this book
is available from the British Library.

This One High Field receives financial assistance
from the Arts Council.

Contents

Division *page* 11
Net 12
The Mooncalves 13
Elsewhere 14
Black Sun 15
Rent 16
Hijacking the Hare 17
Cut to an Echo 18
What Was Mistook 20
Hand to the Stove 21
Émigré, Golders Green 22
Last Things 23
The Lumber Room
   SAPWOOD 25
   HEARTWOOD 25
   PITHWOOD 25
Novice 27
In Convex 28
Endpoint 29
Transparencies 30
Solstice 31
Three-fold
   ON METAPHORS 32
   BARRACKLIKE 32
   FORGE 33
White Hyacinth, Cut Glass 34
The Difficult Balance 35
Timepiece 36
The Old Ice House 37
Townlands 38
The Measure 43
Making Room 44
Blue for a Wonder 45
Carte Blanche 46
Annex 47
Eclipse 48

Abuttals 49
Three Sevens
   EAST 50
   WEST 50
   ØRESUND BRIDGE 50
Wrest 51
Unwitting 52
On Assertions 53
Outrun 55
Rootstalks 56
Sargasso 57
Marker 58

Acknowledgements 60

THIS ONE HIGH FIELD

Division

There are woodlands where it's always dusk,
treetops pinch the light before it chances to enter,
commonplace browns and purples are let radiate.

Galaxy in flux, no bottom or edge, no real harbour
to speak of — yet nothing quite runs asunder,
direction becomes a tablet under the tongue.

Mutable terrors are replaced with a softer kind,
maybe motherly or grandmother-like; a rapture
from a different century.

Sometimes the children ask if all terrors are the same.
The elders preserve — the deep-set question
pursued and put to the back of the mind.

Net

Chimney smoke impaled the sky.
And the nothingness afterward.
The roof and its defeated blue.
Cold-rolled frost and stars.

Window blinds collapsed an outside world.
Lamplight minus the dark suggested remains.
A wet-cheeked face searched for nests,
for warbles in small fields of sleep.

The Mooncalves

Light had released its press of thumb-to-wrist
and lay in the amplitude of its pulse.
For a time it was un-persistent. Capacious.

The sun hadn't yet gone down. It pocketed
its watch and stole to the hills,
mountains that made a border.

They didn't see the thinned man, key
in hand, scurrying to and fro from the lock —
the fillip to this run of unmarked silver.

Elsewhere

They were hidden, the unexposed clefts;
indistinguished water ran to flatter ground.

There was a garlic-rich scent, close but distant.
From a small pool one fish surfaced and flared silver.

But we'd left it too late —
the gold we travelled with had been milled

to a graphite dust, the car and the meadow we'd left
it beside, bossed pewter.

The moon thinned for veins in unyielding trees,
summer gibberish issued from autumn's tongue.

Night swallowed us whole.
We were silent for the drive back.

Black Sun

There was something absurd in the cold and the quiet,
those mute hours of anger, how I'd thought I'd taught myself
to quicken, quicken in the way a murmuration of starlings
quickens, hastens to higher speeds of flight seen in sepia
or black against blue, a seamlessness of utter abandon
working an illusion or sleight of suspense of having no air
between one body and another; that no matter the number
when one changes direction so do the others.
The Danes call this *sort sol*.

Rent

Autumn with its hands between knees and head bent
as if to listen for softened ticks that might rise from a wrist
or to something heard-in-distance, maybe news that a line
will be delayed. And the rift, the sudden rent in its cloudwork:

as when a child throws a half-eaten apple and the bruised
core is momentarily exposed like a gulf; the underbright
that follows — as outside an awning when radiance floods
but is blunted making a read of things only able for uncertainties.

Hijacking the Hare

I turn from field and distant star.
Cold furs and envelops — it is hand-
sewn and threaded with beadwork.

My lungs are filled with nightsong,
the soot of violets, heart-thawed,
flight prized to a pocket.

Luminous again.
Sky-lift, a fraction from land's parallel.
Something near or akin to waking.

This quiet obscure: breath just visible
and the sudden clear beauty of black
ice abstracted by strong light.

Cut to an Echo

Indistinct, night wearies itself into day
and dawn comes to with an early bruise lacking yellow.

A bird falters to redden its song, a snag of notes that can't lift.
The scalded teapot brews darkly and intensely hot.

There is nothing to be done. Not now.
The kitchen and its workable parts have neared to a standstill.

You must lift the cozy from the room's cold, to your cup.
You must pour yourself the hottest drop.

⌁

A different county, this.
No road home —

but a road back,
a place where you can put your head.

It's all context, the heart of the matter,
even if you're loathe to name it: the sight and no sight

of you, face behind your hands; cinched breath,
a stone pillow wedged at your chest.

⌁

The translator posted his version of events.
An almost-there account, a nearly-but-not-nearly-but-not-quite,

his words a framework for the woman who lived
inside them; every image captured through a window.

For all they said and didn't say.
Silhouettes on stone, on glass, on wood.

The shadow that made a question of your mouth.
The music heard from other rooms.

What Was Mistook

The road that kept close to the coast.
The field that kept from the road.
The weighted length of spring.

The stream that opened a hand.
The hill that opened to a shoulder.
The drunk-remorse of summer.

The sun that packed in its fairground.
The woodland that packed copper with gold.
The hound at the heel of autumn.

The wind that looked to recede.
The hoar that looked only hale.
The studded mouth of winter.

Hand to the Stove

The note she said she didn't write is here.
And it says the impossible possibilities
have burned themselves to the quick:
like pressing my hand to the stove
and keeping it there.

Even when she said she couldn't say
what had been done, the head's failures
or the heart's triumphs or vice versa:
it's all the same, a burthen of rotten
wood that won't burn.

Her voice edging casual, edging pain —
thinned black words unable to bend
their weight:
I keep pressing my hand to the stove,
but it's cold. And I can't burn.

Émigré, Golders Green

We'd meet early morning, a softer hour likened to dusk.
Come, come, she'd say, gesturing to the half-dark, the gate.
To the moon armchaired entertaining neither win nor defeat.

∽

Some mornings there was no pretence. Nor moon.
Each of us a curve at the curve of a world. As if we were
a pause, a figuring out. Pair-imperfect, toiled at half-proofs.

∽

A comfort, our brief illusion of enclosure, the lawn with its sole
discretion of familial blues and yellows. *I remember the garden
at night. I have mistaken you.* She said these two things only once.

Last Things

The robin's cold blood is livid.
The hawthorn, a barcode;
the red ink of her breast
mars the data.

∾

A teardrop, the island's design.
And its grassland inclined to bald
or grow blind; the misprison
of briar's dog rose.

∾

The unsweetened beauty
of that wild deer and the dead root-
tendril hanging from her still warm
stiffening face.

∾

A quenched light in a storm
lantern and the river smoked.
Wind soldiering up and down.
Unexpected birdsong.

∾

An hour's diminishing territory.
Unenclosed space lit as a dark
auditorium. Almost a nullity
but for the light step of stars.

∾

I'm unclear if I know the language
or if I've lost my tongue —
I must lay myself down, barren
my head to this groundswell.

The Lumber Room

SAPWOOD

The sea commands from a drowned floor,
greyhauled, abstract as molten glass —
though there's no feel to the wind at all.

Behind you a burr of hills.
And this grist of light sharpening light,
the breadth of a grindstone.

You let your eye rest. And wait.
Cormorants dive and disappear.
Unseen hands are ripping silk.

HEARTWOOD

In the deeper part of the forest you find the coldest
expanse of floor — an unwaxed table, mute
asterisks of moss.

Hidden from stars, there's a faceless dark.
A dark like no dark before.
Somewhere a stag's foot has jutted against roots.

Night has motioned to walk with you.
One side of its hand is gold, the other onyx.
You have refused the offer.

PITHWOOD

How faithful grief is, returning
to remind in the stillness
of near everything gone —

its picked-up slack tick
muscle-tensed, oxygen-
desperate,

like the figure of a woman
who has just kissed the dawn
and is making her way indoors.

Novice

after Walter Frederick Osborne

Faceless to us, their expressions are concealed
by the oils they wear. We see in profile a bob
and heavy fringe, an unflushed cheek.

Animated and resembling the dressed-up figures
she schools, there's this little earth-pink fist
that roused a piped fold from her skirt.

The bed is overgrown, a makeshift lawn.
And she's kneeling as if bending toward a secret,
mouthed from the face a flower.

She cannot feel us,
eyes pressed to read a thought,
full of pasts and thinking of futures.

Sunlight comes and goes.
The wind is blue. Fruit trees
will be coming into bloom.

In Convex

I swim with purpose
to a midpoint.
Only to wade.

The river's blacked out.
From the moon's unsteady
hand, a swinging lantern.

I follow the oxygen-green lack
of pattern, and the music that plays
so low: reed, a little wind, tree.

There is the presence
of another here, as if
in an adjoining room.

Bulb unclothed, an eighty-
watt globe allows to see more
clearly what's to be done.

Endpoint

I was river beneath a field
near an orchard
where fruit bloomed and fell.

When I moved it was mostly
to my own accord.
Sometimes weather insisted.

From my mouth a low-lovely
talk that solitudists
came to endear;

inland, I was touched —
the mind's after-the-fact,
loved like a sacrament.

I was gift, a spell, a thread.
You were the cast net,
a hope.

Transparencies

Winter unlooses the lost and undergrown,
releases in spates cannier spaces found in wood.
There is a patience, a whittling to necessity;
how it cultivates, specifically hand-turns,
another side of contentment.

∽

Light occupies the unpeopled house. It rubs
its weightless hands together and looks to look
deeper inside. The way a stranger might.
All the airs of keeping watch. The soothing kind.
What else can it do?

Solstice

Like a sick animal, he noises and turns
in and out of sleep.

Twice he's turned to the door
mistaking a presence there.

As a tide repeats, he breaks quietly.
His loss weeps alone.

⤳

He doesn't notice, pool trickling
the edge of his feet,

the spilled creel, the new air —
day's arrival like a bright, blank note.

Forgotten. And not. Like the cuckoo,
heard yesterday, out of eyeshot.

I watch him as I would a shadow.
Sunlight cuts a line between the pair of us.

Three-fold

ON METAPHORS

I ought to have thought
better of calling in again.
I could have let go

where we were,
the afternoon expiring,
the sun on the ruin,

those untroubled words
that fell from the sky's idiom.

My thoughts wearied at the task.
They are so faithless.

BARRACKLIKE

Sniper quiet.
A reservoir of noise
zeroes to a pinpoint.

More thought than threat,
the weather's vexed: heat
plays at rain-strings.

The faculty of the eye,
practised at impressions,
takes the view.

A fatigue of blue withstands.
Even this sky fails
to command you.

FORGE

A return to naught.
This breathless little world
is not made for divers like you.

What perishes here
goes.
Even the bones.

Sometimes it's true:
fact refuses the insistence
of certain facts.

White Hyacinth, Cut Glass

And there it was: in the middle
of a winter-dirty frame,

the quiet of the avenue further
removed with lack of people or traffic,

lean to slight — its half-coquettish white
more wild hope than soon-to-be-dead;

the gleam of its green-silver stem
like a pin with a loose clasp —

the well water, the cut glass
displacing the flycatcher, the striplight;

all the clatter, all the dark,
the impossible back and forth.

The Difficult Balance

I'd thought we were going to count cattle.
You were weather-anxious, vexed.
And left before I knew you'd gone.

From the back door, the distance of three
fields, there was the shot of the back
of your hand. How well you heard my call.

I caught up as you were overing a wall,
maybe I was laughing or winded or both,
my arm going out to protect;

the rage that'd changed you,
the sting of your face: a too hot lamp,
a fire that jumped.

The summon, of instinct, to turn and walk
and the difficult balance of the sense of self
that stayed.

Timepiece

I return to wind it
to believe time
still exists here.

If I took the clock,
or let it be left
or right twice,

I'd have no reason
to revisit; I'm aware
of the key

I hold and what is
disturbed by
its presence.

The Old Ice House

Reduced to a sleepless solitude,
a single gable poised as a blue heron.
                    It gleams,
then passes to shadow.

Hardly a tree in sight, the wide field
sways its long, grass skirt;
                    shell and gravel
hem the sea's expanse.

Rain-occasioned, there's the fern
and sheen of an otherwise grey relief;
                    the smoked glass
estuary hasn't mended torn sheets.

Such mute violence in ice.
Yet there's hardly a whisper of that today,
                    a pale warmth
lends from stone —

petrol and foxglove, tipped ash
pastel fissures of quiet that exist here;
                    and sometimes
the wind softens like an old courtesy.

Townlands

It is windless, or nearly. Now and again
there's a sift or a creak, unsteady movements
lift from the field's frame. Little lights blot
the damped chalk skyline.

The estuary haunts, its voice intense
as it lows from a blind spot, disagreed
words or a harsh verse rising.

Repeatedly turning to the river for more
or less river, these narrow sweeps that widen
and widened sweeps that narrow. Constant,
consistent, all flux. Daylit and gaunt, the beech

trees are beaded with rooks, thinned sentries
and the air triggered to still: cut gun
metals inspected with sunlight.

⁓

Wind-tousle and kiss at what's left of a chimney's
mouth. A cairn of ash losing form in the grate.
Irradiated sheepshit and weather-scoured stone.

This place and its fleet of secrets — how is it that
it's like a child upped from bed and having lost being
frantic is content to walk not in search of a parent?

An alcove above a broken staircase,
space cleared for the sky to be
hung just so —

as if the thoughtful hand of a curator had brushed
the smaller details: wanton knots undone
and the execution of weeds in certain gaps.

~

A reproach of shorebirds and the estuary.
Wind-browsed grass and water, the shore-
edged pink house.

There are the maybes — a mending of things
blighted: stones not quite sunk and window-lights
snuffed to dark; a porthole here, another there,
like the simper of a hurt child's breath.

A handshake of lambs run from hooped stars
of barbed wire. And part moon-dressed,
the unassertive white branches of birch.

Further out, blue islanded.
Black-green as the sea's floor.
Day upturned, it has forgotten
it was ever here.

~

In the Protestant cemetery a new grave does not
feign shallow or hollow. Set at a rise, it merges
with shadow to blur light.

There are jackdaws that have yet to come downstairs.
Un-nested but clustered, they watch from stripped
balconies in grey shirts and black suits.

Unequivocal the deep voice of silence and the estuary
talking over it; grievings heard come and go,
the gravediggers hang back and smoke.

A morning that's tried to shape itself from root
and thorn, clots of mud and leaf — matter set and hardened
by a rounder distant glare, as if it were a solid thing.

⤳

The river's slow work. Angles shelved and richly curved,
quiet incandescent turns, grotto dark and unclear.
We try to listen, or imagine we do —

for the hum of a razor or a scale coming loose,
for the feel of something: cold air perhaps
shouldering warm skin.

But it's a chalked geometry — imprecisions
of cloud in a sky freighting darkness east.
Slowed trains of thought lumbering space,

strangely deep and miles from anywhere.
And the river sounding with the sound of the road,
older acoustics of breath and hoof.

⤳

Past darkfall, mid-river. No human voice for miles.
The estuary that knows no sleep determines
itself to be still.

A tireless cold, in element, without posture;
this small entirety amplified, an unsullied
bedlam minus the noise.

The old boundaries impress, these undersize
dictatorships; to move elsewhere, maybe even drift —
this far in, elsewhere doesn't exist.

Breadth emptied: the has-been of the wreak,
and when the wreck's been cleared.
There's the one door: and it's ajar —

slag on the hardware and jamb.
What to do with the unsummoned hours.
The brackish substance, your gritted hands.

<p>

Night bit with cold.
As if scalded and salt-rinsed.
Moon in the vista
a small hard fist.

I moved from the top of the drive.
There was an uphill road
not far from here
that was said to end in sky.

I went for miles.
Some hand or other
signed this way or that,
but the road kept turning away.

Reason, the sadist said,
brought you to this edge.

<p>

The quay sleeps,
moves to its own
lulled time, a small
boat lit with moon
and wave.

Streams fuller now run
with the blundering cold
and plunged to the elbows
arthritic hedgerows
plead for tonics.

A smoke of citrus green
rubs stark from the trees —
I meet your spring self
transient as a flower
from a hellebore.

The Measure

Such stillness. And the mouth
of the ditch caught in moonlight.

Monk-quiet, earth-dark bangles
incite silver and red.

This meander: furrowed scar
all breath-shine and mineral smell,

bark just stripped,
stones sparked like metal,

and the tether of a low-voltage current,
air-stung trees on this one high field.

Making Room

Stood in a low depression, almost out
of the wind's flow. A page, a measure
of knee-deep green and water heard
but not seen.

Maybe you've been dwelling here
all this time, not in silence as such
but more an indeterminate
structure of sky and air.

It might have been what was
needed, and as good as a cave —
the effort to find
where land doesn't lie.

Blue for a Wonder

I lie in the shadow of the tree at the front of the house.
The new grass that touches my shoulder is spider-soft.
A 4.00 p.m. sun scattershots the hedgerow of lilacs.

Birdsong finds me in clues and snippets. And disappears
unresolved. A glimpsed-at peaceable sense
only a heifer makes when grazing.

∼

The neighbour's roses have been abandoned
for another year. Guiltless, I cut long stems of those
I favour and bring an armful of their rednesses home.

Sometimes I imagine a tap running, or a woman
admiring the suddenness of a sun-darkened room;
I know that space hasn't been lived in for years.

∼

An older threshold. And the repeated study
of the outside bright. Minutes pass
before a reflection is visible.

Like an animal that's become aware,
it disappears when I go to touch —
my hand rests in that dark.

Carte Blanche

June. And summer begins
to dress outside closed rooms.
Bright tangibles, green clarified
brown and sea-white closer to blue.
The darkened strip of lawn that's grown
into the seam where tree and wall meet
is death-still.

Yet there are these hours.
Days consecutively sunburst, small fires
startling orange from auburn:
not since childhood
have I felt so light,
brief intervals when the heart
knows no grief.

Annex

The small lamp waxes the room.
Gold first, then blue. Like the postcard
that arrived this morning, stamped

and franked but void of a word or two —
a space that hasn't been filled
with language yet.

One side of the window
reflects a near-clearness
of objects, mirrors without meaning
to; how well the other side knows

to keep shtum. I wake to this room
a thousand times over and wait
for a tongue to fall from the roof
of its mouth.

Eclipse

An accountable order. The timber left to dry
beside the coal shed uncharmed an evening rain;
the months-not-cut grass lay sodden. There'd been
the night-birds, their pale songs ascending
from the strand. And further along the estuary story-
telling between river and sea and field.
                              Back door locked
and black-hooded lamp beside the kettle turned off,
the split in the breadboard was obscured by jars
disinterred from a field in Kilmessan. Abridged to fractional,
slighting to narrow, everything relatively night-hushed —
like a part-calved ice block threatening a surface.

Abuttals

Children heard earlier have fallen silent.
I lean, put my ear closer to the water:
damp minnows so lightly to rest on my skin,
a marginal give.

∿

This magnitude — the unkempt meadows and wind.
Beyond, the bight drones like an engine submerged.
I am compelled toward the moon-cooled tarmac,
its negative space.

∿

I can't hear it rightly, the dream-talk rising:
the populated shore between wake and sleep;
sometimes the tide doesn't claim but salvages
a metal-worked taste.

∿

Scalp-close as I am, there's the urge to feel for
the drum of lungwork; the urge is pressed elsewhere,
touching everything, not touched by anything,
night taps a blind hand.

Three Sevens

for Evelyn

EAST

Late spring in Malmö in our rain-tattered lives.
Yellows and blues appear in kind and lift the flatter land.
From the balcony we watch sleep-nooked birds
in the highest point of the lindens and the woman
who must descend flights to stand out of doors to smoke.
More often than not I hear you humming.
I am not oblivious to your thoughts.

WEST

A parade of bicycles. The backcloth of sea and red tiles.
Beyond courtyards, we enclose ourselves to smaller
secure rooms — alive to what might be movement.
Stilled worlds in portraiture and landscape. Footfall
and weather occasion to intrude; crosscurrents of words
float. We imagine interiors against our own,
darker spaces we don't yet know.

ØRESUND BRIDGE

The train's stalled. The queue has amassed to a crowd.
I know you want me to enquire. Yet I know you know
that we're okay to wait. The sea is fog-choked.
And the bridge. Sun-behind-cloud efforts to press on.
You stare through the carriage glass and steel
in the absence of being moved.
Or what I think is an absence of being moved.

Wrest

The draining board's inherent interim: copper
pans, rinsed plates and cups; tap restrained,
an inset light lifts mute from Belfast enamel.
And the windows reinvesting dark, with love
and other things, to thrive at night as makeshift
mirrors. Sometimes there's an archaic face that swims
in and out of wavelength — akin to a miner quarrying
for air or lost headgear, a half-remembered interior;
what woman hasn't stood and stared while drying
ringless hands, un-absentminded as she burns
a green cloth into her palms? No apprentice
to what-nots or nothings, an ear at work to prise
sound, to root at the corresponding somethings.

Unwitting

A mistake, realized too late, my refusal
to leave or break up the house sooner.
I'd thought of it last summer, weeks spent

clearing loft and sheds, when you asked,
fork pitched at a load of extinguished rubble,
what were you thinking?

I understood what you meant but either had
or hadn't the heart to explain or answer.
Later, looking again at a photograph

restored to a cleaner mantel, the edge
of us dulled by too strong a flash or light-
damaged from ledge-spent years,

the speculation of those smaller, stubborn
details: the wilted flowers, the half-eaten cake,
the permanent grease stains, the wish-blown wax.

On Assertions

We were at the same window.
You looking out and I, in.

The sill between us glazed in frost
at eye level, and the late winter light.

We'd been struggling to find our feet for the better
part of the season, maybe longer;

despite insulation, and other efforts to extract
cold from rooms (midday fires, bled radiators)

the house, as if repelled, would not take to the heat.
Though it breathed it was insensibly numb.

I was sealing one of the sitting-room windows,
a job I'd thought done last summer.

The gun for the sealant had broken. I'd made do
by having sawed the tube and applying at a snail's pace

with a slim bent knife. There was the consolation of a draught
expelled, but I wasn't sure: with gloves, my hands couldn't

reach the narrow space and now, without, they'd become
barely moveable, bloodied at the knuckles.

I'd wished at that moment, looking in at your face, to quit.
To let the coming evening move me to less low ground,

benign and open as the space I was sealing.
Later, after you'd gone to bed, I turned the blinds

to let night in. On the face of it the window
was as it was earlier: glassy, immobile.

But I knew it was minus the draught,
the exposed space filled with sealant

that was probably still in the process
of becoming set.

Outrun

I'd gone up the back for kindling as much to clear my head
as to gather starters for the fire. Maybe a complicated
pleasure given the day's mildness.

I stood in the tree-line and tried to root my feet closer to roots
I couldn't see. Dense browns and greens like slivers of scraped
and flaked paint; age-stained silver. And the fencerow beyond

only seen in glimpses. There was a complicit feel, something
hard-won, an understory's completeness. I wanted to think
that there was no more than this, that I'd left my devotions

at the back door or the top of the drive. But the coal bucket
was empty. And the kindling untouched. I waited a while
longer before gathering a small storm for the fire.

Rootstalks

We are reassembling, our brief appraisals
from the front step twined and bound unevenly.
I'm still here, you've naturally moved on;
each return, this is what you tell me
you'll miss.

Evening has thinned, the moon at the back
of the house hasn't reached us yet. An off-note
hush has found its last piece and settled. Further on
slow flourishes form and reform, sway-waves
from the atmosphere.

A blue argument rends and releases: a push
forward, a turning away and in spells, a stasis.
What is it that makes me think of Bashō?
Drunk. Running down a mountain.
Petals sticking and unsticking to his soles.

There's only so much that can be possessed.

Sargasso

A table's appearance: bread and breadknife, spoon and cup.
The kettle chiming with the opening of a book.

Here a dense spine. There a sinuous horizon.
The *An Post* van arrives and departs.

Morning everywhere. First-hand whites.
Irises loosening signal-yellow tongues.

And the air with its alkaline taste —
startled, a heart declares something matters.

Marker

A canvas disfigured
by a dark scar of cloud,

and the scar both
opening and afterward;

the architecture of trees
old but hopeful,

the constant farewells,
summer-empty rooms.

Acknowledgements

Acknowledgements are due to the editors of the following publications where a number of these poems, or versions of them, were published first: *Magma, The Manchester Review, The Meniscus Review, Poetry International, Poetry Ireland Review* and *Poetry Review*. My thanks to Peter Fallon and all at The Gallery Press. And to the Arts Council/An Chomhairle Ealaíon for the generosity of a grant. To Vona Groarke — for the good nature of kindnesses, for which I am indebted. Most of all, my thanks to the loveliest two people I know: Evelyn and Hugh.